INTRODUCTION

Fires can be very dangerous. All over the world, men and women are specially trained to fight fires in all sorts of places. These can be far out at sea, up tall buildings or deep in forests. Fire-fighters are also involved in other types of emergency. They often have to rescue people trapped underground and even deal with flooding.

Ladders
The tender carries ladders. These are used to rescue people from high buildings – or to get a cat out of a tree!

Water outlet
Fire-fighters attach hoses to the water outlets. These are found all over the fire tender.

Equipment
The fire tender carries hoses, lights, first-aid equipment, breathing equipment (*see* page 16) and fire-fighters' axes.

Control panel
The control panel operates the pump that pushes water along the hoses.

FIRE TENDER
Fire tenders race down streets to get to a blaze. Their lights are flashing and sirens are blaring to clear a path through traffic.

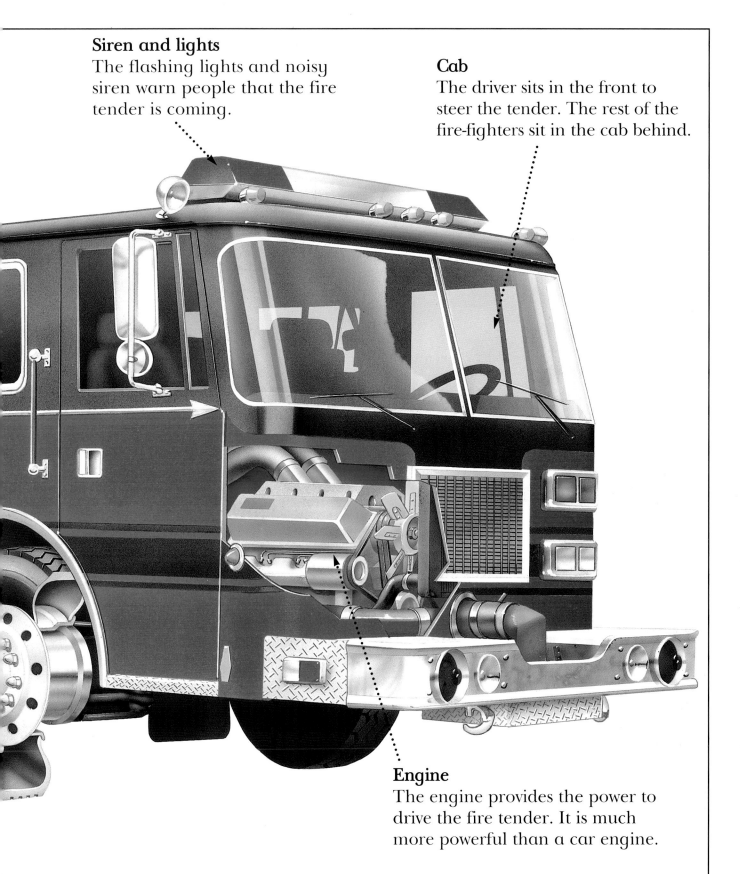

Siren and lights
The flashing lights and noisy siren warn people that the fire tender is coming.

Cab
The driver sits in the front to steer the tender. The rest of the fire-fighters sit in the cab behind.

Engine
The engine provides the power to drive the fire tender. It is much more powerful than a car engine.

The tender carries a team of fire-fighters. It also holds all the equipment they need to cope with many situations.

This includes a big tank full of water. This holds enough water to fill over 40 baths! The water is pumped out through the hoses.

Fire tenders come in

Steam tender

Early fire tenders were powered by steam (*left* and *below*). Water was heated in a boiler to produce steam. This gave the tender's pump the power to push water through the hoses.

Seat

Boiler

1863

Wheel

all shapes and sizes.

Today's tenders

This tiny fire tender (*left*) carries ladders, hoses and two fire-fighters. It can get to fires down very narrow streets.

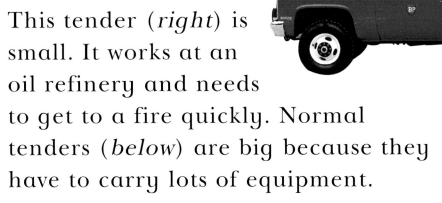

This tender (*right*) is small. It works at an oil refinery and needs to get to a fire quickly. Normal tenders (*below*) are big because they have to carry lots of equipment.

Turntable

The ladder is fitted to a turntable. This can spin the ladder in a complete circle. The end of the ladder can also move up and down.

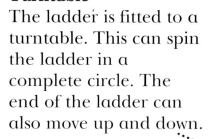

Stabiliser
These special legs stop the fire truck from falling over when the ladder is used.

AERIAL TILLER

Sometimes, fire-fighters need to reach fires in high places. To do this they use a long ladder.

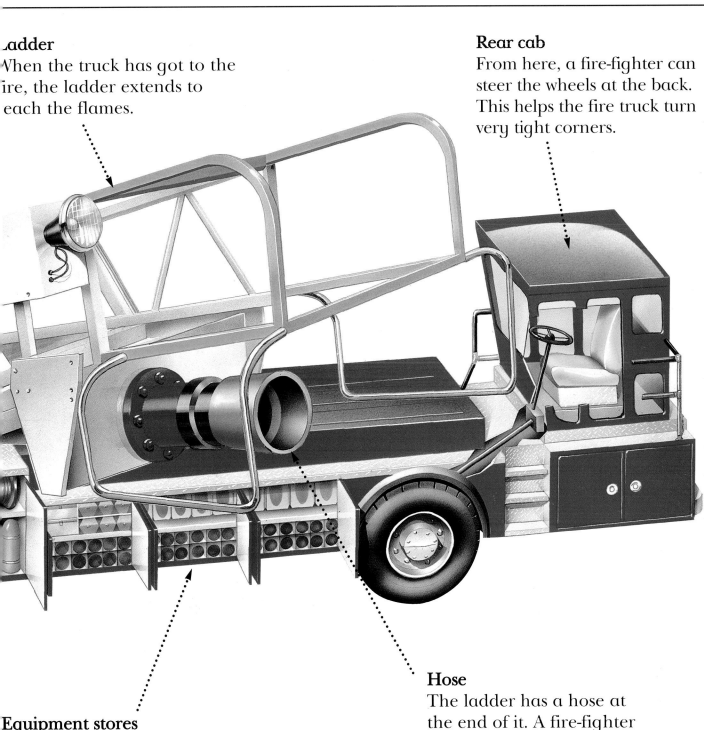

Ladder
When the truck has got to the fire, the ladder extends to reach the flames.

Rear cab
From here, a fire-fighter can steer the wheels at the back. This helps the fire truck turn very tight corners.

Equipment stores
Fire-fighters need a lot of equipment to put out a fire. This fire truck has lots of space under the ladder to store all the gear they use.

Hose
The ladder has a hose at the end of it. A fire-fighter can use this hose to put out fires in high places.

This fire truck has a very long ladder. It is as tall as 20 people standing on top of each other! There is also a cab where the fire-fighters sit. Even though it is very long, this fire truck can get down winding streets because its back can swing around.

Fire-fighters can get

Ladder rescue

People can get trapped in tall burning buildings. To rescue them, fire-fighters climb up a long ladder and help the people back down to safety (*left*).

High hoses

The hose on the end of a ladder lets fire-fighters spray water at flames that are far beyond the range of hoses on the ground (*below*).

Dropping in

Sometimes, even the longest ladder is not long enough. If this happens, fire-fighters may have to climb down the side of a building to reach a blaze (*above*).

to very high places.

Platform

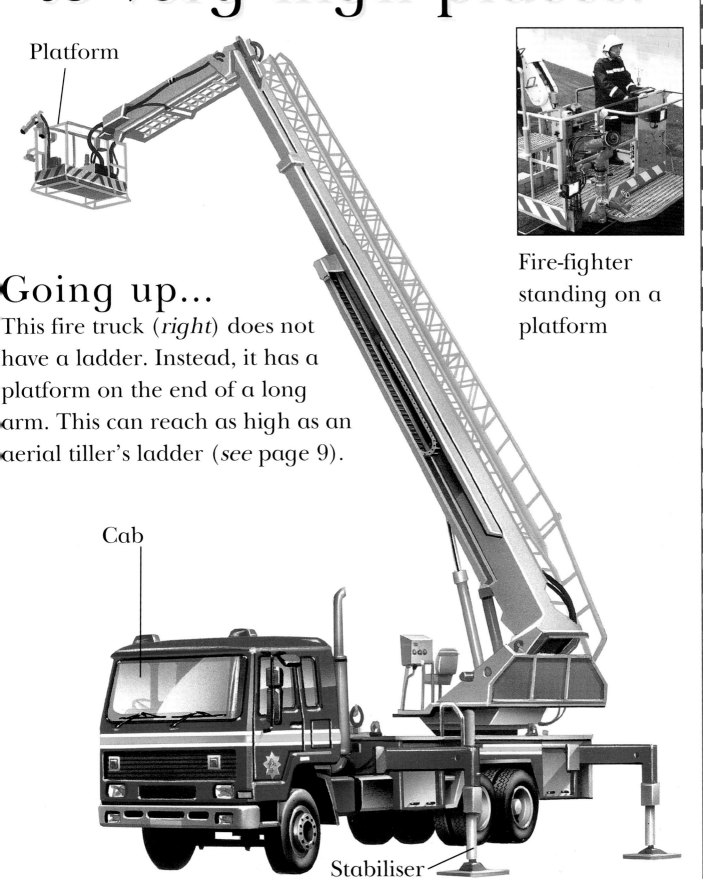

Fire-fighter standing on a platform

Going up...

This fire truck (*right*) does not have a ladder. Instead, it has a platform on the end of a long arm. This can reach as high as an aerial tiller's ladder (*see* page 9).

Cab

Stabiliser

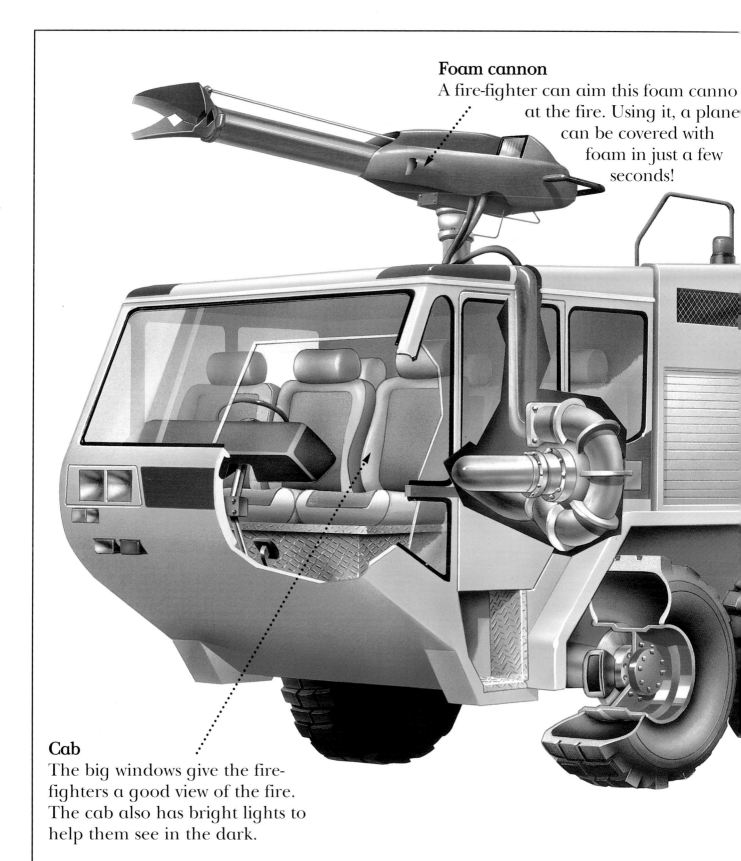

Foam cannon
A fire-fighter can aim this foam canno
at the fire. Using it, a plane
can be covered with
foam in just a few
seconds!

Cab
The big windows give the fire-
fighters a good view of the fire.
The cab also has bright lights to
help them see in the dark.

AIRPORT TENDER

Fires at airports can be very dangerous.
Disasters can happen in just a few seconds
because aircraft fuel burns very easily.

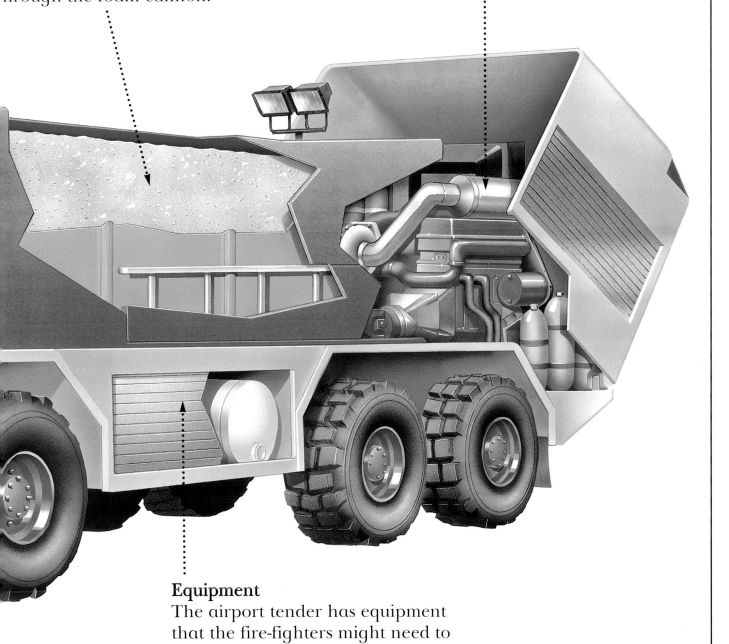

Foam tank
Foam is stored in a huge tank inside the airport tender. From here, a powerful pump forces foam out through the foam cannon.

Engine
The engine is very powerful. It has to drive the tender at high speed and power the pump.

Equipment
The airport tender has equipment that the fire-fighters might need to rescue people from a burning plane. This includes ladders and breathing equipment.

When it arrives at a fire, the airport tender covers the blaze with a thick blanket of foam. Foam is used because water would not stop aircraft fuel from burning. The tender is always on alert, because planes are always landing at busy airports.

Different emergencies

Off-road tender

This fire truck (*left*) can drive over rough ground. It carries a small water tank. It also has a pump that can take water from lakes or ponds.

Rescue truck

Not all emergencies are fires. This truck (*right*) has a crane to lift heavy objects. It also carries equipment to rescue people trapped in cars or even underground.

Shine a light!

This fire truck (*left*) has very bright lights. These are fixed to a pole that can be raised high above the truck. This helps fire-fighters see during an emergency.

need different trucks.

Crane

Stabiliser

Command cab

Some fires are very big and need many fire-fighters to put them out. To direct such operations, a fire chief uses a special truck (*below*). This has a cab at the rear that acts as a command centre.

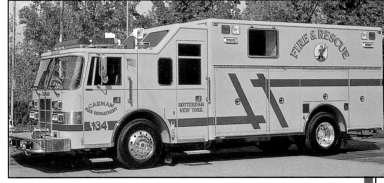

Extra foam

At very big fires, extra foam may be needed. The foam carrier (*right*) carries enough spare foam to help put out the largest of fires.

What it takes to

On standby

A lot of a fire-fighter's time is spent waiting for the next emergency. If the alarm goes when they are eating (*left*), they have to leave their food.

Into action

Fire-fighters need to act quickly when the alarm goes. Sometimes, they slide down a pole (*right*) to get to their fire trucks as quickly as possible. Every second counts!

Safe breathing

Fire-fighters protect themselve from smoke and fumes by wearing equipment (*left*) that gives them air to breathe.

be a fire-fighter.

Cleaning up

Sometimes, fire-fighters don't have to tackle a blaze. They may have to clean up some dangerous chemicals. To do this, they wear special suits (*left*).

Be prepared

After an emergency, fire-fighters have to clean and check all their equipment (*right*). They then get ready for the next alarm...

Cab
The front cab is fitted with sirens, flashing lights and a radio. It can carry three fire-fighters and the driver.

Equipment
There are fire-extinguishers and breathing equipment in the front cab. It also holds stretchers and a first-aid kit.

Tracks
Instead of wheels, this tender has tracks. These help it to drive over very rough ground.

TRACKED TENDER
This tender is used to get to fires in hard-to-reach places. It can drive through a muddy field, and even travel through rivers!

Foam tank
The rear cab holds a large tank. This contains foam that the fire-fighters use to put out a blaze.

More equipment
The rear cab holds rescue equipment, ladders, a pump and some hoses.

However, the ground may be too rough even for this tender. If this happens, it can be picked up and flown to a fire by helicopter.

Although they are small, the cabs of the tender can carry a team of fire-fighters and the equipment they need to tackle a blaze.

Fighting fires in

Guarding the tunnel

Specially built fire trucks (*right*) are used in the Channel Tunnel, which runs between England and France. These trucks drive down a rescue tunnel to reach a fire on a train.

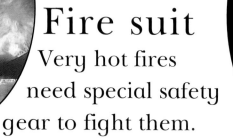

Fire suit

Very hot fires need special safety gear to fight them. This suit (*above left*) protects fire-fighters from high-temperature fires.

Oil-well fire

At an oil-well fire, fire-fighters put up barriers to protect themselves (*left*). When they stand behind these, they are shielded from the heat of the flames.

strange places.

Fire marshal

Racing cars can catch fire because they carry lots of fuel. As a result, motor races have their own special fire-fighters (*below*). If there is a fire, they will put out the flames and rescue the driver.

Robot fire-fighter

This robot fire-fighter (*right*) is used to get to fires that human fire-fighters couldn't reach. These could be in very small spaces or in places too dangerous for people.

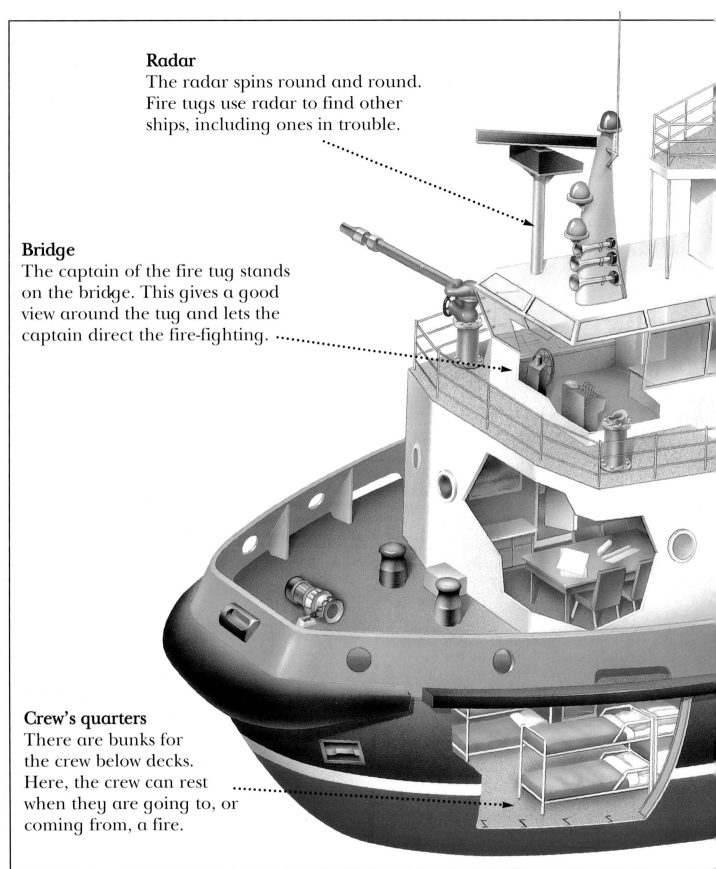

Radar
The radar spins round and round.
Fire tugs use radar to find other
ships, including ones in trouble.

Bridge
The captain of the fire tug stands
on the bridge. This gives a good
view around the tug and lets the
captain direct the fire-fighting.

Crew's quarters
There are bunks for
the crew below decks.
Here, the crew can rest
when they are going to, or
coming from, a fire.

FIRE TUG

Fire tugs fight fires on ships and oil-rigs.
They also tackle blazes that are on land,
at ports, harbours and along rivers.

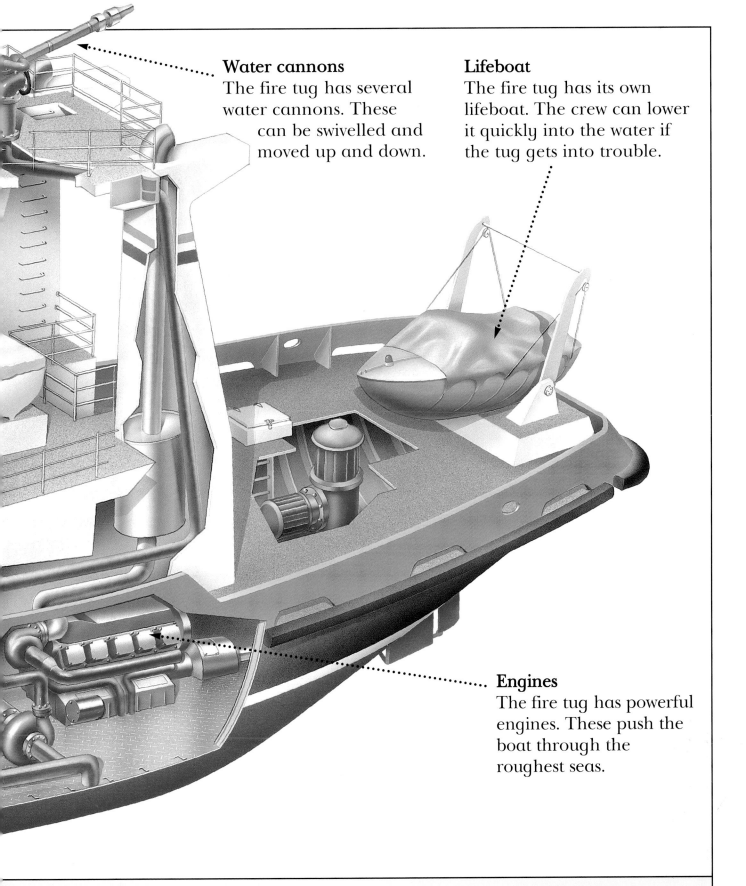

Water cannons
The fire tug has several water cannons. These can be swivelled and moved up and down.

Lifeboat
The fire tug has its own lifeboat. The crew can lower it quickly into the water if the tug gets into trouble.

Engines
The fire tug has powerful engines. These push the boat through the roughest seas.

The captain guides the boat close to the fire. The tug then pumps sea- or river-water out through its water cannons.

These throw out massive jets of water that spray over long distances – up to the length of a football pitch!

Fires at sea can be

Support at sea

This huge craft (*right*) is called an Emergency Support Vessel (ESV). It is used to fight serious fires on oil-rigs. It has helicopters to rescue people and cranes to lift objects out of the water.

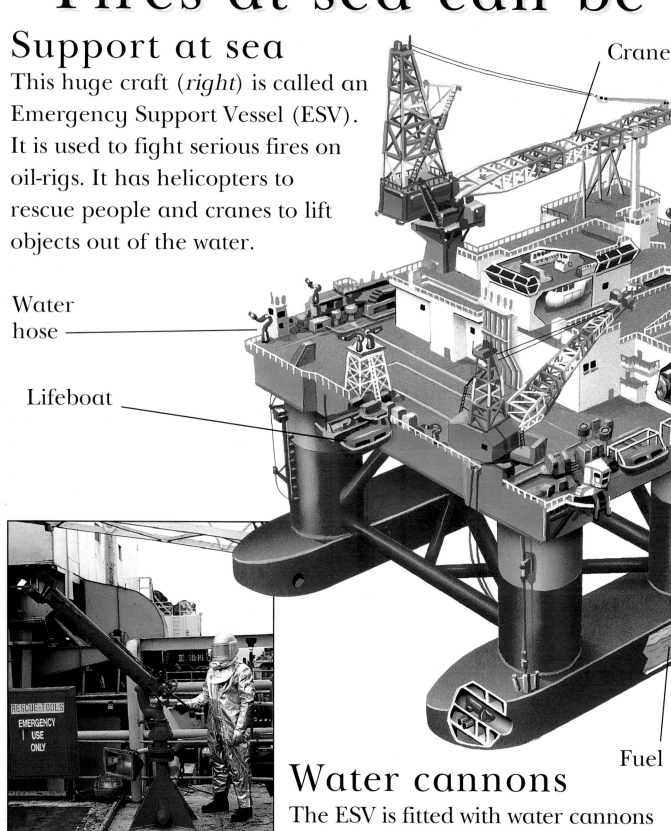

Crane

Water hose

Lifeboat

Fuel

Water cannons

The ESV is fitted with water cannons (*left*). These special hoses are similar to those on a fire tug (*see* pages 22-23).

RESCUE-TOOLS
EMERGENCY
USE
ONLY

very dangerous.

Oil-rig fires

Fires on oil-rigs (*left*) are very fierce. This is because the oil and gas rushes up very quickly from the seabed. This makes the fire very difficult to put out.

Helicopter

Powerful jets

The huge jets of water from a fire tug's cannons show how powerful its pumps are (*right*).

Propeller

Coastguard

When a fire occurs on a small boat, the coastguard may respond to the alarm (*left*). They have fast boats that can rescue people before a blaze gets out of control.

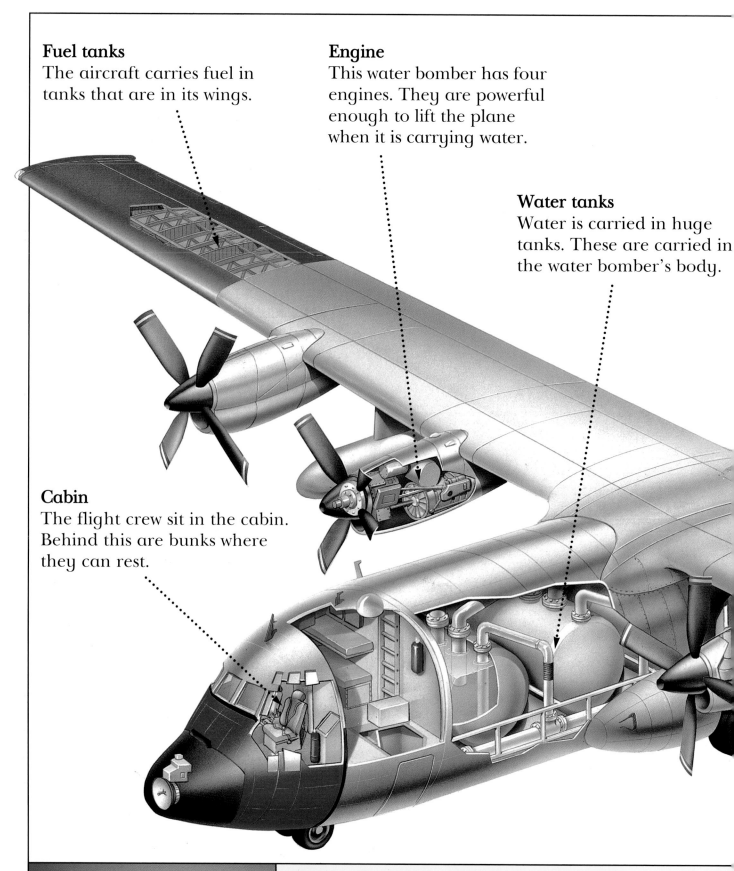

Fuel tanks
The aircraft carries fuel in tanks that are in its wings.

Engine
This water bomber has four engines. They are powerful enough to lift the plane when it is carrying water.

Water tanks
Water is carried in huge tanks. These are carried in the water bomber's body.

Cabin
The flight crew sit in the cabin. Behind this are bunks where they can rest.

WATER BOMBER

A water bomber is an aircraft that can drop water on a fire. It is used to fight forest fires, especially in areas that are hard to reach.

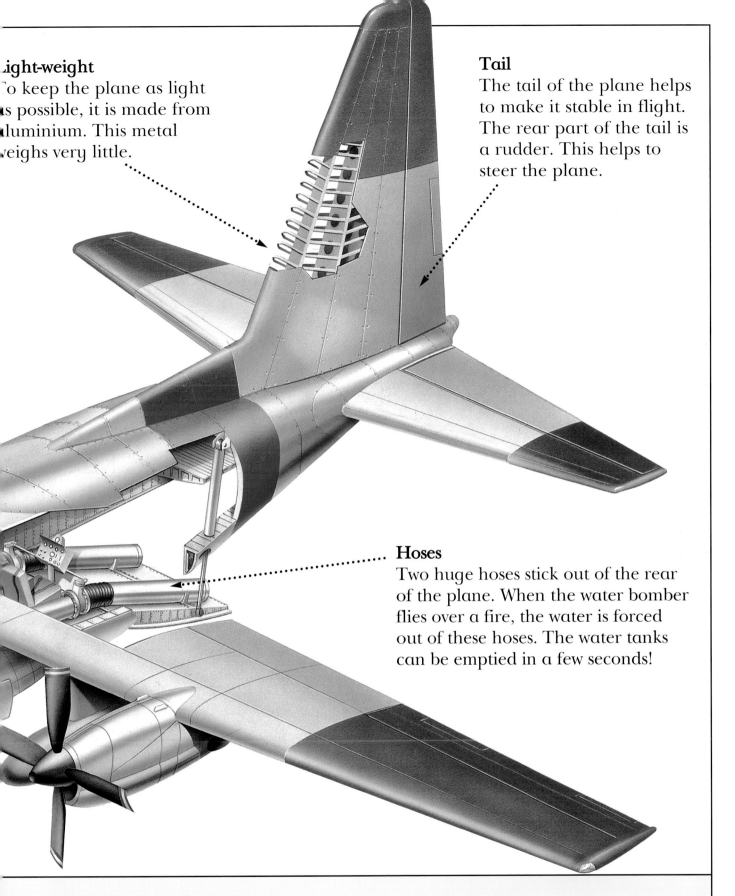

Light-weight
To keep the plane as light as possible, it is made from aluminium. This metal weighs very little.

Tail
The tail of the plane helps to make it stable in flight. The rear part of the tail is a rudder. This helps to steer the plane.

Hoses
Two huge hoses stick out of the rear of the plane. When the water bomber flies over a fire, the water is forced out of these hoses. The water tanks can be emptied in a few seconds!

The aircraft flies low over a fire. With one pass, the plane can spray water over a large area of burning woodland.

The water bomber then returns to its airfield. Here, it refills its tanks with more water, before flying back to fight the fire.

There are many ways

Jumping into fires

Some fire-fighters are trained to parachute close to forest fires (*left*). This is useful when they are needed in a hurry at fires that are hard to reach.

Beating fires

Fire-fighters often try to beat out a forest fire (*below*). This is a good way to fight fires where no water is available.

Starting fires

Some fires are started deliberately (*above*). By burning forest scrub in a controlled way, fire-fighters can prevent serious forest fires from spreading.

to fight forest fires.

Helicopters

Helicopters can hover over the site of a fire. They drop water from a bucket which they carry beneath (*right*).

Water bucket

Forest tender

Special tenders carry firefighters to forest fires (*right*). They are built to drive over rough ground.

Fantastic Facts

• The first organised fire brigade was in ancient Rome. The fire-fighters were equipped with hand pumps, ladders, buckets and pickaxes. They also had blankets to protect them from heat.

• In 1982, a fire in Borneo lasted for 10 months. It was only put out when heavy rain started to fall.

• In the summer of 1988, a forest fire at Yellowstone National Park, USA, burned about half the park's area. At one time, nearly 9,500 fire-fighters were used to tackle the blaze.

• Smoke kills more people than fire itself. This is why breathing equipment is so important in helping to fight fires and rescue people trapped in a blaze.

Glossary

Aerial tiller

A fire truck that can be steered from the rear as well as the front, like the tiller of a ship.

Breathing equipment

A device that supplies air to a facemask worn by fire-fighters. This lets them breathe in a smoke-filled room.

Coastguard

An organisation that watches the coastline to prevent accidents and smuggling.

Fire tender

A fire truck that carries a tank containing its own supply of water or foam.

Siren

A device fitted to a fire-fighting vehicle that makes a wailing sound. This warns people that fire-fighters are coming.

Track

A loop that runs around wheels, helping a vehicle move over rough ground.

Turntable

The base on which a ladder rests. It allows the ladder to turn in a circle.

Water cannon

A special device fitted to a fire tug or ESV. It is used to point a jet of water at a fire.

Index

PHOTO CREDITS
Abbreviations; t-top, m-middle, b-bottom, r-right, l-left

Pages 4, 10b, 16 both, 17t, 20m, 28b & 29b – Shout Pictures. 6t – Hulton Getty Collection. 7tl – Rex Features. 7tr, 11, 14 both, 15b & 18 – Angloco Ltd. 7b, 8 & 15m – Pierce Manufacturing. 10t, 24 & 25m – Eye Ubiquitous. 10m, 12, 20b, 20-21, 21b, 22, 25t & b, 26, 28t & 28-29 – Frank Spooner Pictures. 16b – Spectrum Colour Library. 17b – Science Photo Library. 21m – Empics.